The Yoga

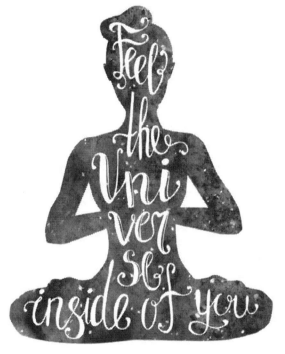

Notebook

By: ROSEANNE BAKER

www.breakthroughempire.com

The Yoga

Notebook

♥ Created with a splash of glitter and inspiration ♥

ROSEANNE BAKER

Founder of Breakthrough Empire™

ISBN-13:
978-1974311729

ISBN-10:
1974311724

This notebook
belongs to the
incredibly fabulous:

If found, please call:

First, she fell in ♥ love with her yoga. Then, she fell in love with herself.

Today's Date: _____

Yoga heals the soul. Just breathe and know that you are loved. ♥

Today's Date: _____

Yoga heals the soul. Just breathe and know that you are loved. ♥

_____
_____
_____
_____
_____
_____
_____
_____
_____
_____
_____
_____
_____
_____
_____
_____
_____
_____
_____
_____
_____
_____
_____
_____
_____
_____
_____

Today's Date: _____

Yoga heals the soul. Just breathe and know that you are loved. ♥

Today's Date: _____

Yoga heals the soul. Just breathe and know that you are loved. ♥

_____
_____
_____
_____
_____
_____
_____
_____
_____
_____
_____
_____
_____
_____
_____
_____
_____
_____
_____
_____
_____
_____
_____
_____
_____

Today's Date: _____

Yoga heals the soul. Just breathe and know that you are loved. ♥

_____
_____
_____
_____
_____
_____
_____
_____
_____
_____
_____
_____
_____
_____
_____
_____
_____
_____
_____
_____
_____
_____
_____
_____
_____
_____
_____

Today's Date: _____

Yoga heals the soul. Just breathe and know that you are loved. ♥

_____

_____

_____

_____

_____

_____

_____

_____

_____

_____

_____

_____

_____

_____

_____

_____

_____

_____

_____

_____

_____

_____

_____

Today's Date: _____

Yoga heals the soul. Just breathe and know that you are loved. ♥

Today's Date: _____

Yoga heals the soul. Just breathe and know that you are loved. ♥

Today's Date: _____

Yoga heals the soul. Just breathe and know that you are loved. ♥

_____

_____

_____

_____

_____

_____

_____

_____

_____

_____

_____

_____

_____

_____

_____

_____

_____

_____

_____

_____

_____

_____

_____

_____

_____

Today's Date: _____

Yoga heals the soul. Just breathe and know that you are loved. ♥

_____

_____

_____

_____

_____

_____

_____

_____

_____

_____

_____

_____

_____

_____

_____

_____

_____

_____

_____

_____

_____

_____

_____

Today's Date: _____

Yoga heals the soul. Just breathe and know that you are loved. ♥

_____
_____
_____
_____
_____
_____
_____
_____
_____
_____
_____
_____
_____
_____
_____
_____
_____
_____
_____
_____
_____
_____
_____
_____

Today's Date: _____

Yoga heals the soul. Just breathe and know that you are loved. ♥

_____

_____

_____

_____

_____

_____

_____

_____

_____

_____

_____

_____

_____

_____

_____

_____

_____

_____

_____

_____

_____

_____

_____

_____

Today's Date: _____

Yoga heals the soul. Just breathe and know that you are loved. ♥

Today's Date: _____

Yoga heals the soul. Just breathe and know that you are loved. ♥

_____
_____
_____
_____
_____
_____
_____
_____
_____
_____
_____
_____
_____
_____
_____
_____
_____
_____
_____
_____
_____
_____
_____
_____

Today's Date: _____

Yoga heals the soul. Just breathe and know that you are loved. ♥

_____
_____
_____
_____
_____
_____
_____
_____
_____
_____
_____
_____
_____
_____
_____
_____
_____
_____
_____
_____
_____
_____
_____
_____

Today's Date: _____

Yoga heals the soul. Just breathe and know that you are loved. ♥

_____
_____
_____
_____
_____
_____
_____
_____
_____
_____
_____
_____
_____
_____
_____
_____
_____
_____
_____
_____
_____
_____
_____
_____
_____
_____
_____
_____
_____

Today's Date: _____

Yoga heals the soul. Just breathe and know that you are loved. ♥

Today's Date: _____

Yoga heals the soul. Just breathe and know that you are loved. ♥

_____

_____

_____

_____

_____

_____

_____

_____

_____

_____

_____

_____

_____

_____

_____

_____

_____

_____

_____

_____

_____

_____

_____

_____

Today's Date: _____

Yoga heals the soul. Just breathe and know that you are loved. ♥

Today's Date: _____

Yoga heals the soul. Just breathe and know that you are loved. ♥

_____
_____
_____
_____
_____
_____
_____
_____
_____
_____
_____
_____
_____
_____
_____
_____
_____
_____
_____
_____
_____
_____
_____
_____
_____

Today's Date: _____

Yoga heals the soul. Just breathe and know that you are loved. ♥

_____
_____
_____
_____
_____
_____
_____
_____
_____
_____
_____
_____
_____
_____
_____
_____
_____
_____
_____
_____
_____
_____
_____
_____

Today's Date: _____

Yoga heals the soul. Just breathe and know that you are loved. ♥

_____
_____
_____
_____
_____
_____
_____
_____
_____
_____
_____
_____
_____
_____
_____
_____
_____
_____
_____
_____
_____
_____
_____
_____
_____

Today's Date: _____

Yoga heals the soul. Just breathe and know that you are loved. ♥

Today's Date: _____

Yoga heals the soul. Just breathe and know that you are loved. ♥

_____
_____
_____
_____
_____
_____
_____
_____
_____
_____
_____
_____
_____
_____
_____
_____
_____
_____
_____
_____
_____
_____
_____
_____
_____
_____

Today's Date: _____

Yoga heals the soul. Just breathe and know that you are loved. ♥

_____
_____
_____
_____
_____
_____
_____
_____
_____
_____
_____
_____
_____
_____
_____
_____
_____
_____
_____
_____
_____
_____
_____
_____
_____
_____
_____
_____
_____
_____

Today's Date: _____

Yoga heals the soul. Just breathe and know that you are loved. ♥

_____
_____
_____
_____
_____
_____
_____
_____
_____
_____
_____
_____
_____
_____
_____
_____
_____
_____
_____
_____
_____
_____
_____
_____
_____

Today's Date: _____

Yoga heals the soul. Just breathe and know that you are loved. ♥

_____
_____
_____
_____
_____
_____
_____
_____
_____
_____
_____
_____
_____
_____
_____
_____
_____
_____
_____
_____
_____
_____
_____
_____
_____

Today's Date: _____

Yoga heals the soul. Just breathe and know that you are loved. ♥

_____
_____
_____
_____
_____
_____
_____
_____
_____
_____
_____
_____
_____
_____
_____
_____
_____
_____
_____
_____
_____
_____

Today's Date: _____

Yoga heals the soul. Just breathe and know that you are loved. ♥

_____
_____
_____
_____
_____
_____
_____
_____
_____
_____
_____
_____
_____
_____
_____
_____
_____
_____
_____
_____
_____
_____
_____
_____
_____

Today's Date: _____

Yoga heals the soul. Just breathe and know that you are loved. ♥

_____
_____
_____
_____
_____
_____
_____
_____
_____
_____
_____
_____
_____
_____
_____
_____
_____
_____
_____
_____
_____
_____
_____

Today's Date: _____

Yoga heals the soul. Just breathe and know that you are loved. ♥

Today's Date: _____

Yoga heals the soul. Just breathe and know that you are loved. ♥

_____
_____
_____
_____
_____
_____
_____
_____
_____
_____
_____
_____
_____
_____
_____
_____
_____
_____
_____
_____
_____
_____
_____
_____
_____

Today's Date: _____

Yoga heals the soul. Just breathe and know that you are loved. ♥

_____
_____
_____
_____
_____
_____
_____
_____
_____
_____
_____
_____
_____
_____
_____
_____
_____
_____
_____
_____
_____
_____
_____
_____
_____
_____
_____
_____
_____
_____
_____

Feel the Universe inside of you

Today's Date: _____

Yoga heals the soul. Just breathe and know that you are loved. ♥

_____
_____
_____
_____
_____
_____
_____
_____
_____
_____
_____
_____
_____
_____
_____
_____
_____
_____
_____
_____
_____
_____
_____
_____
_____
_____
_____
_____

Today's Date: _____

Yoga heals the soul. Just breathe and know that you are loved. ♥

_____

_____

_____

_____

_____

_____

_____

_____

_____

_____

_____

_____

_____

_____

_____

_____

_____

_____

_____

_____

_____

_____

Today's Date: _____

Yoga heals the soul. Just breathe and know that you are loved. ♥

_____
_____
_____
_____
_____
_____
_____
_____
_____
_____
_____
_____
_____
_____
_____
_____
_____
_____
_____
_____
_____
_____
_____
_____
_____

Today's Date: _____

Yoga heals the soul. Just breathe and know that you are loved. ♥

_____
_____
_____
_____
_____
_____
_____
_____
_____
_____
_____
_____
_____
_____
_____
_____
_____
_____
_____
_____
_____
_____
_____
_____
_____
_____
_____
_____
_____

Feel the Universe inside of you

Today's Date: _____

Yoga heals the soul. Just breathe and know that you are loved. ♥

Today's Date: _____

Yoga heals the soul. Just breathe and know that you are loved. ♥

_____
_____
_____
_____
_____
_____
_____
_____
_____
_____
_____
_____
_____
_____
_____
_____
_____
_____
_____
_____
_____
_____
_____

Today's Date: _____

Yoga heals the soul. Just breathe and know that you are loved. ♥

_____
_____
_____
_____
_____
_____
_____
_____
_____
_____
_____
_____
_____
_____
_____
_____
_____
_____
_____
_____
_____
_____
_____
_____
_____

Today's Date: _____

Yoga heals the soul. Just breathe and know that you are loved. ♥

Today's Date: _____

Yoga heals the soul. Just breathe and know that you are loved. ♥

_____
_____
_____
_____
_____
_____
_____
_____
_____
_____
_____
_____
_____
_____
_____
_____
_____
_____
_____
_____
_____
_____
_____
_____

Today's Date: _____

Yoga heals the soul. Just breathe and know that you are loved. ♥

_____
_____
_____
_____
_____
_____
_____
_____
_____
_____
_____
_____
_____
_____
_____
_____
_____
_____
_____
_____
_____
_____
_____

Feel the Universe inside of you

Today's Date: _____

Yoga heals the soul. Just breathe and know that you are loved. ♥

_____
_____
_____
_____
_____
_____
_____
_____
_____
_____
_____
_____
_____
_____
_____
_____
_____
_____
_____
_____
_____
_____
_____
_____

Today's Date: _____

Yoga heals the soul. Just breathe and know that you are loved. ♥

_____
_____
_____
_____
_____
_____
_____
_____
_____
_____
_____
_____
_____
_____
_____
_____
_____
_____
_____
_____
_____
_____
_____
_____
_____
_____
_____
_____

Feel the Universe inside of you

Today's Date: _____

Yoga heals the soul. Just breathe and know that you are loved. ♥

_____
_____
_____
_____
_____
_____
_____
_____
_____
_____
_____
_____
_____
_____
_____
_____
_____
_____
_____
_____
_____
_____
_____
_____
_____
_____

Today's Date: _____

Yoga heals the soul. Just breathe and know that you are loved. ♥

_____
_____
_____
_____
_____
_____
_____
_____
_____
_____
_____
_____
_____
_____
_____
_____
_____
_____
_____
_____
_____
_____
_____
_____

Today's Date: _____

Yoga heals the soul. Just breathe and know that you are loved. ♥

_____

_____

_____

_____

_____

_____

_____

_____

_____

_____

_____

_____

_____

_____

_____

_____

_____

_____

_____

_____

_____

_____

Today's Date: _____

Yoga heals the soul. Just breathe and know that you are loved. ♥

_____
_____
_____
_____
_____
_____
_____
_____
_____
_____
_____
_____
_____
_____
_____
_____
_____
_____
_____
_____
_____
_____
_____
_____
_____
_____
_____
_____

Today's Date: _____

Yoga heals the soul. Just breathe and know that you are loved. ♥

_____
_____
_____
_____
_____
_____
_____
_____
_____
_____
_____
_____
_____
_____
_____
_____
_____
_____
_____
_____
_____
_____

Today's Date: _____

Yoga heals the soul. Just breathe and know that you are loved. ♥

Feel the Universe inside of you.

Today's Date: _____

Yoga heals the soul. Just breathe and know that you are loved. ♥

_____
_____
_____
_____
_____
_____
_____
_____
_____
_____
_____
_____
_____
_____
_____
_____
_____
_____
_____
_____
_____
_____
_____
_____
_____
_____
_____
_____

Today's Date: _____

Yoga heals the soul. Just breathe and know that you are loved. ♥

Today's Date: _____

Yoga heals the soul. Just breathe and know that you are loved. ♥

_____
_____
_____
_____
_____
_____
_____
_____
_____
_____
_____
_____
_____
_____
_____
_____
_____
_____
_____
_____
_____
_____
_____
_____
_____

Today's Date: _____

Yoga heals the soul. Just breathe and know that you are loved. ♥

Today's Date: _____

Yoga heals the soul. Just breathe and know that you are loved. ♥

_____
_____
_____
_____
_____
_____
_____
_____
_____
_____
_____
_____
_____
_____
_____
_____
_____
_____
_____
_____
_____
_____
_____
_____

Today's Date: _____

Yoga heals the soul. Just breathe and know that you are loved. ♥

_____
_____
_____
_____
_____
_____
_____
_____
_____
_____
_____
_____
_____
_____
_____
_____
_____
_____
_____
_____
_____
_____
_____
_____
_____

Feel the Universe inside of you

Today's Date: _____

Yoga heals the soul. Just breathe and know that you are loved. ♥

_____
_____
_____
_____
_____
_____
_____
_____
_____
_____
_____
_____
_____
_____
_____
_____
_____
_____
_____
_____
_____
_____
_____
_____
_____
_____

Today's Date: _____

Yoga heals the soul. Just breathe and know that you are loved. ♥

Today's Date: _____

Yoga heals the soul. Just breathe and know that you are loved. ♥

_____
_____
_____
_____
_____
_____
_____
_____
_____
_____
_____
_____
_____
_____
_____
_____
_____
_____
_____
_____
_____
_____
_____
_____
_____
_____
_____
_____

Today's Date: _____

Yoga heals the soul. Just breathe and know that you are loved. ♥

_____
_____
_____
_____
_____
_____
_____
_____
_____
_____
_____
_____
_____
_____
_____
_____
_____
_____
_____
_____
_____
_____
_____
_____
_____

Today's Date: _____

Yoga heals the soul. Just breathe and know that you are loved. ♥

_____
_____
_____
_____
_____
_____
_____
_____
_____
_____
_____
_____
_____
_____
_____
_____
_____
_____
_____
_____
_____
_____
_____
_____
_____
_____
_____

Today's Date: _____

Yoga heals the soul. Just breathe and know that you are loved. ♥

_____
_____
_____
_____
_____
_____
_____
_____
_____
_____
_____
_____
_____
_____
_____
_____
_____
_____
_____
_____
_____
_____
_____
_____
_____

Today's Date: _____

Yoga heals the soul. Just breathe and know that you are loved. ♥

_____
_____
_____
_____
_____
_____
_____
_____
_____
_____
_____
_____
_____
_____
_____
_____
_____
_____
_____
_____
_____
_____
_____
_____
_____

Today's Date: _____

Yoga heals the soul. Just breathe and know that you are loved. ♥

_____
_____
_____
_____
_____
_____
_____
_____
_____
_____
_____
_____
_____
_____
_____
_____
_____
_____
_____
_____
_____
_____
_____
_____
_____
_____
_____
_____

Today's Date: _____

Yoga heals the soul. Just breathe and know that you are loved. ♥

_____
_____
_____
_____
_____
_____
_____
_____
_____
_____
_____
_____
_____
_____
_____
_____
_____
_____
_____
_____
_____
_____
_____
_____
_____

Today's Date: _____

Yoga heals the soul. Just breathe and know that you are loved. ♥

Today's Date: _____

Yoga heals the soul. Just breathe and know that you are loved. ♥

_____
_____
_____
_____
_____
_____
_____
_____
_____
_____
_____
_____
_____
_____
_____
_____
_____
_____
_____
_____
_____
_____

Today's Date: _____

Yoga heals the soul. Just breathe and know that you are loved. ♥

_____
_____
_____
_____
_____
_____
_____
_____
_____
_____
_____
_____
_____
_____
_____
_____
_____
_____
_____
_____
_____
_____
_____
_____
_____
_____

Today's Date: _____

Yoga heals the soul. Just breathe and know that you are loved. ♥

_____

_____

_____

_____

_____

_____

_____

_____

_____

_____

_____

_____

_____

_____

_____

_____

_____

_____

_____

_____

_____

_____

Today's Date: _____

Yoga heals the soul. Just breathe and know that you are loved. ♥

_____
_____
_____
_____
_____
_____
_____
_____
_____
_____
_____
_____
_____
_____
_____
_____
_____
_____
_____
_____
_____
_____
_____
_____

Feel the Universe inside of you

Today's Date: _____

Yoga heals the soul. Just breathe and know that you are loved. ♥

_____
_____
_____
_____
_____
_____
_____
_____
_____
_____
_____
_____
_____
_____
_____
_____
_____
_____
_____
_____
_____
_____
_____
_____
_____
_____

Today's Date: _____

Yoga heals the soul. Just breathe and know that you are loved. ♥

_____
_____
_____
_____
_____
_____
_____
_____
_____
_____
_____
_____
_____
_____
_____
_____
_____
_____
_____
_____
_____
_____
_____
_____
_____
_____

Today's Date: _____

Yoga heals the soul. Just breathe and know that you are loved. ♥

_____
_____
_____
_____
_____
_____
_____
_____
_____
_____
_____
_____
_____
_____
_____
_____
_____
_____
_____
_____
_____
_____
_____
_____
_____

Today's Date: _____

Yoga heals the soul. Just breathe and know that you are loved. ♥

Today's Date: _____

Yoga heals the soul. Just breathe and know that you are loved. ♥

_____
_____
_____
_____
_____
_____
_____
_____
_____
_____
_____
_____
_____
_____
_____
_____
_____
_____
_____
_____
_____
_____
_____

Today's Date: _____

Yoga heals the soul. Just breathe and know that you are loved. ♥

Today's Date: _____

Yoga heals the soul. Just breathe and know that you are loved. ♥

_____
_____
_____
_____
_____
_____
_____
_____
_____
_____
_____
_____
_____
_____
_____
_____
_____
_____
_____
_____
_____
_____
_____
_____
_____
_____
_____

Feel the Universe inside of you.

Today's Date: _____

Yoga heals the soul. Just breathe and know that you are loved. ♥

_____
_____
_____
_____
_____
_____
_____
_____
_____
_____
_____
_____
_____
_____
_____
_____
_____
_____
_____
_____
_____
_____
_____
_____

Today's Date: _____

Yoga heals the soul. Just breathe and know that you are loved. ♥

_____
_____
_____
_____
_____
_____
_____
_____
_____
_____
_____
_____
_____
_____
_____
_____
_____
_____
_____
_____
_____
_____
_____
_____
_____
_____
_____

Today's Date: _____

Yoga heals the soul. Just breathe and know that you are loved. ♥

Feel the universe inside of you

Today's Date: _____

Yoga heals the soul. Just breathe and know that you are loved. ♥

_____
_____
_____
_____
_____
_____
_____
_____
_____
_____
_____
_____
_____
_____
_____
_____
_____
_____
_____
_____
_____
_____
_____
_____
_____
_____

Today's Date: _____

Yoga heals the soul. Just breathe and know that you are loved. ♥

Today's Date: _____

Yoga heals the soul. Just breathe and know that you are loved. ♥

_____

_____

_____

_____

_____

_____

_____

_____

_____

_____

_____

_____

_____

_____

_____

_____

_____

_____

_____

_____

_____

_____

_____

_____

_____

Today's Date: _____

Yoga heals the soul. Just breathe and know that you are loved. ♥

Today's Date: _____

Yoga heals the soul. Just breathe and know that you are loved. ♥

_____
_____
_____
_____
_____
_____
_____
_____
_____
_____
_____
_____
_____
_____
_____
_____
_____
_____
_____
_____
_____
_____
_____
_____
_____
_____
_____
_____
_____
_____

Today's Date: _____

Yoga heals the soul. Just breathe and know that you are loved. ♥

Today's Date: _____

Yoga heals the soul. Just breathe and know that you are loved. ♥

_____
_____
_____
_____
_____
_____
_____
_____
_____
_____
_____
_____
_____
_____
_____
_____
_____
_____
_____
_____
_____
_____
_____
_____
_____
_____

Today's Date: _____

Yoga heals the soul. Just breathe and know that you are loved. ♥

Today's Date: _____

Yoga heals the soul. Just breathe and know that you are loved. ♥

_____

_____

_____

_____

_____

_____

_____

_____

_____

_____

_____

_____

_____

_____

_____

_____

_____

_____

_____

_____

_____

Today's Date: _____

Yoga heals the soul. Just breathe and know that you are loved. ♥

Today's Date: _____

Yoga heals the soul. Just breathe and know that you are loved. ♥

_____

_____

_____

_____

_____

_____

_____

_____

_____

_____

_____

_____

_____

_____

_____

_____

_____

_____

_____

_____

_____

_____

_____

_____

_____

Today's Date: _____

Yoga heals the soul. Just breathe and know that you are loved. ♥

Today's Date: _____

Yoga heals the soul. Just breathe and know that you are loved. ♥

_____

_____

_____

_____

_____

_____

_____

_____

_____

_____

_____

_____

_____

_____

_____

_____

_____

_____

_____

_____

_____

_____

_____

Today's Date: _____

Yoga heals the soul. Just breathe and know that you are loved. ♥

_____
_____
_____
_____
_____
_____
_____
_____
_____
_____
_____
_____
_____
_____
_____
_____
_____
_____
_____
_____
_____

Feel the Universe inside of you

Today's Date: _____

Yoga heals the soul. Just breathe and know that you are loved. ♥

_____

_____

_____

_____

_____

_____

_____

_____

_____

_____

_____

_____

_____

_____

_____

_____

_____

_____

_____

_____

_____

_____

_____

_____

_____

_____

_____

Today's Date: _____

Yoga heals the soul. Just breathe and know that you are loved. ♥

Today's Date: _____

Yoga heals the soul. Just breathe and know that you are loved. ♥

_____

_____

_____

_____

_____

_____

_____

_____

_____

_____

_____

_____

_____

_____

_____

_____

_____

_____

_____

_____

_____

_____

_____

_____

Today's Date: _____

Yoga heals the soul. Just breathe and know that you are loved. ♥

Feel the Universe inside of you

Today's Date: _____

Yoga heals the soul. Just breathe and know that you are loved. ♥

_____
_____
_____
_____
_____
_____
_____
_____
_____
_____
_____
_____
_____
_____
_____
_____
_____
_____
_____
_____
_____
_____
_____
_____
_____
_____

Today's Date: _____

Yoga heals the soul. Just breathe and know that you are loved. ♥

_____
_____
_____
_____
_____
_____
_____
_____
_____
_____
_____
_____
_____
_____
_____
_____
_____
_____
_____
_____
_____
_____
_____
_____

Today's Date: _____

Yoga heals the soul. Just breathe and know that you are loved. ♥

_____

_____

_____

_____

_____

_____

_____

_____

_____

_____

_____

_____

_____

_____

_____

_____

_____

_____

_____

_____

_____

_____

_____

Today's Date: _____

Yoga heals the soul. Just breathe and know that you are loved. ♥

_____
_____
_____
_____
_____
_____
_____
_____
_____
_____
_____
_____
_____
_____
_____
_____
_____
_____
_____
_____
_____
_____
_____
_____

Today's Date: _____

Yoga heals the soul. Just breathe and know that you are loved. ♥

_____

_____

_____

_____

_____

_____

_____

_____

_____

_____

_____

_____

_____

_____

_____

_____

_____

_____

_____

_____

_____

_____

_____

Today's Date: _____

Yoga heals the soul. Just breathe and know that you are loved. ♥

Today's Date: _____

Yoga heals the soul. Just breathe and know that you are loved. ♥

_____
_____
_____
_____
_____
_____
_____
_____
_____
_____
_____
_____
_____
_____
_____
_____
_____
_____
_____
_____
_____
_____
_____
_____

Today's Date: _____

Yoga heals the soul. Just breathe and know that you are loved. ♥

Today's Date: _____

Yoga heals the soul. Just breathe and know that you are loved. ♥

_____

_____

_____

_____

_____

_____

_____

_____

_____

_____

_____

_____

_____

_____

_____

_____

_____

_____

_____

_____

_____

_____

_____

Today's Date: _____

Yoga heals the soul. Just breathe and know that you are loved. ♥

_____

_____

_____

_____

_____

_____

_____

_____

_____

_____

_____

_____

_____

_____

_____

_____

_____

_____

_____

_____

_____

Today's Date: _____

Yoga heals the soul. Just breathe and know that you are loved. ♥

_____

_____

_____

_____

_____

_____

_____

_____

_____

_____

_____

_____

_____

_____

_____

_____

_____

_____

_____

_____

_____

_____

Today's Date: _____

Yoga heals the soul. Just breathe and know that you are loved. ♥

_____
_____
_____
_____
_____
_____
_____
_____
_____
_____
_____
_____
_____
_____
_____
_____
_____
_____
_____
_____
_____
_____
_____
_____
_____
_____
_____
_____
_____
_____
_____

Feel the Universe inside of you

Today's Date: _____

Yoga heals the soul. Just breathe and know that you are loved. ♥

_____

_____

_____

_____

_____

_____

_____

_____

_____

_____

_____

_____

_____

_____

_____

_____

_____

_____

_____

_____

_____

Today's Date: _____

Yoga heals the soul. Just breathe and know that you are loved. ♥

_____

_____

_____

_____

_____

_____

_____

_____

_____

_____

_____

_____

_____

_____

_____

_____

_____

_____

_____

_____

_____

_____

_____

Today's Date: _____

Yoga heals the soul. Just breathe and know that you are loved. ♥

_____

_____

_____

_____

_____

_____

_____

_____

_____

_____

_____

_____

_____

_____

_____

_____

_____

_____

_____

_____

_____

_____

_____

_____

Today's Date: _____

Yoga heals the soul. Just breathe and know that you are loved. ♥

Today's Date: _____

Yoga heals the soul. Just breathe and know that you are loved. ♥

_____

_____

_____

_____

_____

_____

_____

_____

_____

_____

_____

_____

_____

_____

_____

_____

_____

_____

_____

_____

_____

_____

_____

_____

_____

_____

_____

Today's Date: _____

Yoga heals the soul. Just breathe and know that you are loved. ♥

_____
_____
_____
_____
_____
_____
_____
_____
_____
_____
_____
_____
_____
_____
_____
_____
_____
_____
_____
_____
_____
_____
_____
_____
_____

Feel the Universe inside of you

Today's Date: _____

Yoga heals the soul. Just breathe and know that you are loved. ♥

_____
_____
_____
_____
_____
_____
_____
_____
_____
_____
_____
_____
_____
_____
_____
_____
_____
_____
_____
_____
_____
_____
_____
_____
_____
_____

Today's Date: _____

Yoga heals the soul. Just breathe and know that you are loved. ♥

_____

_____

_____

_____

_____

_____

_____

_____

_____

_____

_____

_____

_____

_____

_____

_____

_____

_____

_____

_____

_____

_____

_____

Today's Date: _____

Yoga heals the soul. Just breathe and know that you are loved. ♥

_____
_____
_____
_____
_____
_____
_____
_____
_____
_____
_____
_____
_____
_____
_____
_____
_____
_____
_____
_____
_____
_____
_____
_____
_____
_____

Today's Date: _____

Yoga heals the soul. Just breathe and know that you are loved. ♥

Today's Date: _____

Yoga heals the soul. Just breathe and know that you are loved. ♥

_____
_____
_____
_____
_____
_____
_____
_____
_____
_____
_____
_____
_____
_____
_____
_____
_____
_____
_____
_____
_____
_____
_____
_____
_____
_____
_____
_____
_____
_____
_____
_____

Today's Date: _____

Yoga heals the soul. Just breathe and know that you are loved. ♥

_____
_____
_____
_____
_____
_____
_____
_____
_____
_____
_____
_____
_____
_____
_____
_____
_____
_____
_____
_____
_____
_____

Today's Date: _____

Yoga heals the soul. Just breathe and know that you are loved. ♥

Feel the Universe inside of you

Today's Date: _____

Yoga heals the soul. Just breathe and know that you are loved. ♥

Today's Date: _____

Yoga heals the soul. Just breathe and know that you are loved. ♥

_____

_____

_____

_____

_____

_____

_____

_____

_____

_____

_____

_____

_____

_____

_____

_____

_____

_____

_____

_____

_____

_____

_____

Today's Date: _____

Yoga heals the soul. Just breathe and know that you are loved. ♥

_____
_____
_____
_____
_____
_____
_____
_____
_____
_____
_____
_____
_____
_____
_____
_____
_____
_____
_____
_____
_____
_____
_____
_____
_____

Today's Date: _____

Yoga heals the soul. Just breathe and know that you are loved. ♥

_____

_____

_____

_____

_____

_____

_____

_____

_____

_____

_____

_____

_____

_____

_____

_____

_____

_____

_____

_____

_____

_____

_____

_____

Today's Date: _____

Yoga heals the soul. Just breathe and know that you are loved. ♥

Today's Date: _____

Yoga heals the soul. Just breathe and know that you are loved. ♥

_____
_____
_____
_____
_____
_____
_____
_____
_____
_____
_____
_____
_____
_____
_____
_____
_____
_____
_____
_____
_____
_____
_____
_____
_____
_____

Today's Date: _____

Yoga heals the soul. Just breathe and know that you are loved. ♥

Today's Date: _____

Yoga heals the soul. Just breathe and know that you are loved. ♥

Feel the Universe inside of you

Today's Date: _____

Yoga heals the soul. Just breathe and know that you are loved. ♥

Today's Date: _____

Yoga heals the soul. Just breathe and know that you are loved. ♥

_____

_____

_____

_____

_____

_____

_____

_____

_____

_____

_____

_____

_____

_____

_____

_____

_____

_____

_____

_____

_____

_____

_____

_____

_____

_____

Today's Date: _____

Yoga heals the soul. Just breathe and know that you are loved. ♥

_____

_____

_____

_____

_____

_____

_____

_____

_____

_____

_____

_____

_____

_____

_____

_____

_____

_____

_____

_____

_____

_____

_____

Today's Date: _____

Yoga heals the soul. Just breathe and know that you are loved. ♥

_____

_____

_____

_____

_____

_____

_____

_____

_____

_____

_____

_____

_____

_____

_____

_____

_____

_____

_____

_____

_____

_____

_____

Today's Date: _____

Yoga heals the soul. Just breathe and know that you are loved. ♥

Today's Date: _____

Yoga heals the soul. Just breathe and know that you are loved. ♥

_____
_____
_____
_____
_____
_____
_____
_____
_____
_____
_____
_____
_____
_____
_____
_____
_____
_____
_____
_____
_____
_____
_____
_____
_____
_____
_____
_____
_____

Feel the Universe inside of you

Today's Date: _____

Yoga heals the soul. Just breathe and know that you are loved. ♥

_____
_____
_____
_____
_____
_____
_____
_____
_____
_____
_____
_____
_____
_____
_____
_____
_____
_____
_____
_____
_____

Feel the Universe inside of you

Today's Date: _____

Yoga heals the soul. Just breathe and know that you are loved. ♥

_____
_____
_____
_____
_____
_____
_____
_____
_____
_____
_____
_____
_____
_____
_____
_____
_____
_____
_____
_____
_____
_____
_____

Feel the Universe inside of you

Today's Date: _____

Yoga heals the soul. Just breathe and know that you are loved. ♥

_____
_____
_____
_____
_____
_____
_____
_____
_____
_____
_____
_____
_____
_____
_____
_____
_____
_____
_____
_____
_____
_____
_____
_____

Today's Date: _____

Yoga heals the soul. Just breathe and know that you are loved. ♥

_____

_____

_____

_____

_____

_____

_____

_____

_____

_____

_____

_____

_____

_____

_____

_____

_____

_____

_____

_____

_____

_____

_____

Today's Date: _____

Yoga heals the soul. Just breathe and know that you are loved. ♥

_____
_____
_____
_____
_____
_____
_____
_____
_____
_____
_____
_____
_____
_____
_____
_____
_____
_____
_____
_____
_____
_____
_____

Today's Date: _____

Yoga heals the soul. Just breathe and know that you are loved. ♥

_____
_____
_____
_____
_____
_____
_____
_____
_____
_____
_____
_____
_____
_____
_____
_____
_____
_____
_____
_____
_____
_____
_____
_____
_____
_____

Today's Date: _____

Yoga heals the soul. Just breathe and know that you are loved. ♥

_____
_____
_____
_____
_____
_____
_____
_____
_____
_____
_____
_____
_____
_____
_____
_____
_____
_____
_____
_____
_____
_____
_____
_____
_____
_____

Feel the Universe inside of you

Today's Date: _____

Yoga heals the soul. Just breathe and know that you are loved. ♥

_____
_____
_____
_____
_____
_____
_____
_____
_____
_____
_____
_____
_____
_____
_____
_____
_____
_____
_____
_____
_____
_____
_____
_____

Today's Date: _____

Yoga heals the soul. Just breathe and know that you are loved. ♥

_____
_____
_____
_____
_____
_____
_____
_____
_____
_____
_____
_____
_____
_____
_____
_____
_____
_____
_____
_____
_____
_____
_____
_____

Today's Date: _____

Yoga heals the soul. Just breathe and know that you are loved. ♥

_____
_____
_____
_____
_____
_____
_____
_____
_____
_____
_____
_____
_____
_____
_____
_____
_____
_____
_____
_____
_____
_____
_____
_____
_____
_____

Today's Date: _____

Yoga heals the soul. Just breathe and know that you are loved. ♥

Feel the Universe inside of you

Today's Date: _____

Yoga heals the soul. Just breathe and know that you are loved. ♥

_____

_____

_____

_____

_____

_____

_____

_____

_____

_____

_____

_____

_____

_____

_____

_____

_____

_____

_____

_____

_____

_____

_____

_____

Well Darn it!

Looks like you've finished up the notebook.
So now, I've gotta ask...

Did you love it ? ♥

If you did, I'd be honored
if you could spread the word and leave a
review on Amazon!

Need another notebook?
I got you covered. ☺
You can find all my books at Amazon by
searching "Roseanne Baker"
Or visit:
http://www.roseannebaker.com

Thank you for your purchase!

xx Roseanne

About the Author

ROSEANNE BAKER is a certified life coach, author, and the founder of breakthroughempire.com. She inspires women to take massive action on their dreams and goals so that they can live lives that truly sparkle.

http://www.roseannebaker.com

Made in the USA
Middletown, DE
08 February 2020